For Ning,
For All the Children,
For Peace and Truth.

"That you are here—that life exists and identity,
That the powerful play goes on, and you may contribute a verse."
-Walt Whitman

There are Worlds within you
My dear child,
Mighty and deep.
You are Vast and Grand,
A Universe Complete.

Oh, no one ever told you so,
In such a simple strand?
Or maybe you've forgotten,
What is always at hand?

Oh Dear,
Let me tell you straight:
You are One with All That Is
And All that Was and Will Be,
Emerged From The Infinite,
And Filled with the Very Same.

Your History is broad and wide,
Connected to humanity,
To Life itself, and growth,
and expansion of mind,
And the Blooming of the World.

Within You
Histories, Cultures, travels vast,
Galaxies,
Geographies and Peoples unique.
Made up of countless Stories you are,
Down a long lineage and line replete.

Cultures converge as mighty rivers in You
Ancestors upon ancestors,
Eons connected to eons,
In You,
Entire Nations Ages and Times!

Did You Know?
Here and Now,
They All Meet In You.

All Meets In You.

Each of us contains so much
No amount of words could tell,
We are much more than we think,
A thoughtful moment of reflection and
Perspective makes this clear:
One level we are an interconnected colony of bugs, microbes;
Another,
Primeval atoms,
Elements forged from stars above.
We are enormous,
We are small,
We are a part of All.

We are All Throughout, Broadcast,
When we see ourselves clear,
Endless Beauty in You, Dear.

Countless aspirations and dreams,
Long held before you,
Blossomed In You.

A tremendous Event we are!
You are!

Living history we are,
Both Ancient and New
Living Nature,
Living Spirit.

"Where does Infinity end and begin?,"
Life asks you, Dearest One.
Where are You then?
How endless the Intelligence
And Wisdom in you,
Around you,
And You Within.

How Beautiful you are!
The Beholder of Lifes Beauty.
How Wonderful you are!
That which wonders Profoundly.
How Timeless your being,
How perfectly in Tune,
How essential to Love You!

Uni-Verse means one Song.
What a Melody you are then,
A Symphony of sorts,
A complex combination,
The Fullness of Love
In One Small Part.

So Sing out your cheery heart,

What a Lovely Mystery You are!

Help Steward:
ECOSIA.ORG

Printed in the USA
CPSIA information can be obtained
at www.ICGtesting.com
CBRC100930271124
18025CB00043B/494